# THE PASSION

BY THE SAME AUTHOR

*Scripture for Meditation: 8*

THE RESURRECTION


IN THE SAME SERIES

*Scripture for Meditation*

INFANCY NARRATIVES
PHILIPPIANS
OUR DIVINE MASTER
COLOSSIANS
CHRISTIAN DEUTERONOMY
FAITH AND REVELATION

*Scripture for Meditation: 7*

# THE PASSION

Henry Wansbrough OSB

 St Paul Publications

**ST PAUL PUBLICATIONS**
SLOUGH   SL3 6BT   ENGLAND

Nihil obstat: Gerald E. Roberts, Censor
Imprimatur: + Charles Grant, Bishop of Northampton
18 January 1973

Printed in Great Britain by the Society of St Paul, Slough
SBN 85439 089 8

# CONTENTS

*ACKNOWLEDGEMENT*

The Bible text in this publication is from the Revised
Standard Version Bible, Catholic Edition, copyrighted ©
1965 and 1966 by the Division of Christian Education of
the National Council of the Churches of Christ in the
U.S.A., and used by permission.

# FOREWORD

The story of our Lord's passion and death is the part of the gospels which took shape earliest, since from the beginning it was a central object of the Christian message. From the earliest times the passion was an object of devotion and meditation by the Christian community. One way in which the narrative of events was enriched was by reference to the Old Testament, since it was the conviction of the early Christians that only in the light of the Old Testament prophecies could the events of the life and death of Jesus be understood.

In the meditations in this booklet the gospel passage which is the subject of meditation is normally put with an Old Testament passage. It was the Old Testament which formed the thought both of Jesus and of the evangelists, so that the New Testament passages can best be understood against this background. In this way we can begin to recapture the richness of thought and the depths of these accounts.

These meditations are offered with hesitation, for reflections of this kind are necessarily personal. It can only be hoped that some thoughts among them may help to start the reader off on reflections of his own, and so issue in prayer.

HENRY WANSBROUGH

Jerusalem
August 1972

# BIBLE PASSAGES USED

## OLD TESTAMENT

## NEW TESTAMENT

# 1

# THE KEY

*Exodus 33:18-23; 34:5-8*

Moses said, "I pray thee, show me thy glory." And he said, "I will make all my goodness pass before you, and will proclaim before you my name 'The Lord'; and I will be gracious to whom I will be gracious, and will show mercy on whom I will show mercy. But," he said, "you cannot see my face; for man shall not see me and live." And the Lord said, "Behold, there is a place by me where you shall stand upon the rock; and while my glory passes by I will put you in a cleft of the rock, and I will cover you with my hand until I have passed by; then I will take away my hand, and you shall see my back; but my face shall not be seen.". . .

And the Lord descended in the cloud and stood with him there, and proclaimed the name of the Lord. The Lord passed before him, and proclaimed, "The Lord, the Lord, a God merciful and gracious, slow to anger, and abounding in steadfast love and faithfulness, keeping steadfast love for thousands, forgiving iniquity and transgression and sin, but who will by no means clear the guilty, visiting the iniquity of the fathers upon the children and the children's children, to the third and the fourth generation." And Moses made haste to bow his head toward the earth, and worshipped.

Now before the feast of the Passover, when Jesus knew that his hour had come to depart out of this world to the Father, having loved his own who were in the world, he loved them to the end.

## Reflection

Here, at the beginning of the story of the passion, John sets the tone of the events. Jesus' actions make sense only as the extreme proof of his love for men. The process of revelation of God's nature and his dealings with man has been a process of the revelation of his love. Right at the beginning, as soon as God admitted Moses to the intimacy of some knowledge of the secret of his being, it is love that is the clue. Throughout the revelation leading up to Christ, Israel is taught more and more clearly of God's love; it is expressed in terms of every family relationship: the love of a father who takes his son in his arms and teaches him to walk 'with leading-strings of love' (Hosea 11), the love of a boy who passionately seeks his girl friend however unfaithful she may be, even greater than the love of a mother who can never forget the fruit of her womb. God's generous and unrequited love is no new discovery of the New Testament, but is the golden thread running through the Old Testament as well.

So at the fullness of time, when Christ comes as the climax of the revelation of God, and shows in human terms the divine nature, it is above all the divine love which he has to translate into a human nature. This is the clue to his dealing with people throughout his ministry, the secret of his ability to draw them, and reaches its climax in the passion. This cannot make sense in terms of appeasement of the wrath of God or the exacting of a penalty for sin, but only as the supreme expression, in a human nature, of love, both the Father's love for men in Christ and Christ's love for, and perfect union with, his Father. We can say what we like about the love God shows to men, but until it is translated into the palpable reality of a man who loves it seems so remote. This is the point of the devotion to the sacred heart, the symbol of Christ's human centre of life and energy. And it is only by reflection on the life and actions of Jesus that we can see how this love of his works out, and so return to some knowledge of the limitless love of God, of which Jesus' love, looked at simply as a human love, is only a translation into a poorer dimension.

**2**

# WASHING THE DISCIPLES' FEET

*Isaiah 52:13—53:12*

Behold, my servant shall prosper,
    he shall be exalted and lifted up,
    and shall be very high.
As many were astonished at him —
    his appearance was so marred,
        beyond human semblance,
    and his form beyond that of the sons of men —
so shall he startle many nations;
    kings shall shut their mouths because of him;
for that which has not been told them they shall see;
    and that which they have not heard
        they shall understand.
Who has believed what we have heard?
    And to whom has the arm of the Lord been revealed?
For he grew up before him like a young plant,
    and like a root out of dry grounds;
he had no form or comeliness that we should look at him,
    and no beauty that we should desire him.
He was despised and rejected by men;
    a man of sorrows, and acquainted with grief;
and as one from whom men hide their faces
    he was despised, and we esteemed him not.
Surely he has borne our griefs
    and carried our sorrows;
yet we esteemed him stricken,
    smitten by God, and afflicted.

But he was wounded for our transgressions,
    he was bruised for our iniquities;
upon him was the chastisement that made us whole,
    and with his stripes we are healed.
All we like sheep have gone astray;
    we have turned every one to his own way;
and the Lord has laid on him
    the iniquity of us all.
He was oppressed, and he was afflicted,
    yet he opened not his mouth;
like a lamb that is led to the slaughter,
    and like a sheep that before its shearers is dumb,
    so he opened not his mouth.
By oppression and judgment he was taken away;
    and as for his generation, who considered
that he was cut off out of the land of the living,
    stricken for the transgression of my people?
And they made his grave with the wicked
    and with a rich man in his death,
although he had done no violence,
    and there was no deceit in his mouth.
Yet it was the will of the Lord to bruise him;
    he has put him to grief;
when he makes himself an offering for sin,
    he shall see his offspring, he shall prolong his days;
the will of the Lord shall prosper in his hand;
    he shall see the fruit of the travail
        of his soul and be satisfied;
by his knowledge shall the righteous one, my servant,
    make many to be accounted righteous;
    and he shall bear their iniquities.
Therefore I will divide him a portion with the great,
    and he shall divide the spoil with the strong;
because he poured out his soul to death,
    and was numbered with the transgressors;
yet he bore the sin of many,
    and made intercession for the transgressors.

Jesus, knowing that the Father had given all things into his hands, and that he had come from God and was going to God, rose from supper, laid aside his garments, and girded himself with a towel. Then he poured water into a basin, and began to wash the disciples' feet, and to wipe them with the towel with which he was girded. He came to Simon Peter; and Peter said to him, "Lord, do you wash my feet?" Jesus answered him, "What I am doing you do not know now, but afterward you will understand." Peter said to him, "You shall never wash my feet." Jesus answered him, "If I do not wash you, you have no part in me." Simon Peter said to him, "Lord, not my feet only but also my hands and my head!" Jesus said to him, "He who has bathed does not need to wash, except for his feet, but he is clean all over; and you are clean, but not all of you." For he knew who was to betray him; that was why he said, "You are not all clean."

When he had washed their feet, and taken his garments, and resumed his place, he said to them, "Do you know what I have done to you? You call me Teacher and Lord; and you are right, for so I am. If I then, your Lord and Teacher, have washed your feet, you also ought to wash one another's feet. For I have given you an example, that you also should do as I have done to you. Truly, truly, I say to you, a servant is not greater than his master; nor is he who is sent greater than he who sent him. If you know these things, blessed are you if you do them."

## Reflection

Before his passion begins Jesus gives a little acted parable by which he shows its meaning: he has come to serve, and is about to give the supreme example of this loving service of his brethren. Peter's horror at this apparent lowering of his master's dignity stands against the background that to wash someone's feet was considered such a debasement that a Hebrew slave could not be obliged to do it — only a gentile slave.

But Jesus, since his baptism in the Jordan, had seen his ministry in terms of the Servant of the Lord prophesied by Isaiah; the predictions of his suffering, especially, are couched in terms which recall Isaiah. The mission of the Servant was to culminate in an act of humiliation by which he would save a great number from their sins and bring them back to God; not only this, but after insult and suffering he himself too would be vindicated. At the moment when his passion was about to begin Jesus must have had this prophecy in mind, and shows by this simple action, an act of loving attention and thoughtful care for his brethren, that he is prepared to carry it out. And yet his perfect balance is remarkable; there is no false humility here; for with complete unpretentiousness he acknowledges that he is Lord and Master, and rightly hailed as such. He has in the highest degree the quality which is so often recognizable in really great men: they are genuinely warmly interested in others, no matter how unimportant; without any condescension they can give themselves to the other and still retain their air of authority. It is only those who are less sure of themselves who have to put up barriers and protections to prevent people prying too deeply into the emptiness that lies within. When one feels empty and inadequate or even hateful for not having the courage to face this, it can be a help to take refuge in the calm adequacy and the unpretentious naturalness of Jesus washing the feet of his disciples. He was Lord and Master but had no fear of abasing himself; his position was clear of itself and he could afford to abandon himself to the demands of serving others, wherever it might lead.

# 3

# THE TRAITOR

*Psalm 41:7-13*

All who hate me whisper together about me;
    they imagine the worst for me.
They say, "A deadly thing has fastened upon him;
    he will not rise again from where he lies."
Even my bosom friend in whom I trusted,
    who ate of my bread, has lifted his heel against me.
But do thou, O Lord, be gracious to me,
    and raise me up, that I may requite them!
By this I know that thou art pleased with me,
    in that my enemy has not triumphed over me.
But thou hast upheld me because of my integrity,
    and set me in thy presence for ever.
Blessed be the Lord, the God of Israel,
    from everlasting to everlasting!
    Amen and Amen.

*Mark 14:18-21*

And as they were at table eating, Jesus said, "Truly, I say to you, one of you will betray me, one who is eating with me." They began to be sorrowful, and to say to him one after another, "Is it I?" He said to them, "It is one of the twelve, one who is dipping bread in the same dish with me. For the Son of man goes as it is written of him, but woe to that man by whom the Son of man is betrayed! It would have been better for that man if he had not been born."

## Reflection

Eating together is a natural symbol of fellowship and forms a further bond. This is even more obvious with the custom at the time of Jesus, when normally there was one central dish round which everyone sat, and from which everyone ate with his fingers. All the twelve dipped into the same dish, which is why all of them can ask, 'Is it I?' In his prediction of the treachery Jesus is not, then, pointing out the traitor, but is underlining the degree of betrayal involved after unity has been expressed so graphically by dipping in the same dish as constantly as the Twelve must have done during all their company with Jesus. One is surprised that this implicit appeal to fidelity did not touch the traitor — until one reflects that the degree of union expressed by dipping into the same dish is surely less than that expressed by the constant sacramental Communion of Christians, and that this does not seem to hinder our betrayals of the Lord and of each other.

This oldest statement of Jesus' plea by the evangelist, later clarified and made more specific by the other evangelists, poses a problem which requires reflection: how much did Jesus know of what was ahead of him? We have no reason to believe that he knew every detail of his sufferings or of his resurrection before they occurred. Formed as he was on the prophecies of the Old Testament, he knew that he must sink to the depths of suffering and humiliation before he was vindicated by his Father, that somehow he would triumph over death. But he had no blueprint of the details; 'a man like us in all things but sin', he must still have suffered the terror of the unknown that lay ahead of him. He could not comfortably calculate just how much suffering there would be or how deep would be his agony — to take a banal example, pain in the dentist's chair is made more bearable by the knowledge that there are only a certain number of teeth to fill — he could only abandon himself totally to his Father. We too are in complete ignorance of what the future may bring, loss of the work we love or of the companions who make life worthwhile, or incapacitating illness. We can, perhaps, prepare to share his disappointment at the traitor.

# 4

# THE COVENANT

*Exodus 12:1-12*

The Lord said to Moses and Aaron in the land of Egypt, "This month shall be for you the beginning of months; it shall be the first month of the year for you. Tell all the congregation of Israel that on the tenth day of this month they shall take every man a lamb according to their father's houses, a lamb for a household; and if the household is too small for a lamb, then a man and his neighbour next to his house shall take according to the number of persons; according to what each can eat you shall make your count for the lamb. Your lamb shall be without blemish, a male a year old; you shall take it from the sheep or from the goats; and you shall keep it until the fourteenth day of this month, when the whole assembly of the congregation of Israel shall kill their lambs in the evening. Then they shall take some of the blood, and put it on the two doorposts and the lintel of the houses in which they eat them. They shall eat the flesh that night, roasted; with unleavened bread and bitter herbs they shall eat it. Do not eat any of it raw or boiled with water, but roasted, its head with its legs and its inner parts. And you shall let none of it remain until the morning, anything that remains until the morning you shall burn. In this manner you shall eat it: your loins girded, your sandals on your feet, and your staff in your hand; and you shall eat it in haste. It is the Lord's passover. For I will pass through the land of Egypt that night, and I will smite all the first-born in the land of Egypt, both man and beast; and on all the gods of Egypt I will execute judgments: I am the Lord."

*Exodus 24:3-8*

Moses came and told the people all the words of the Lord and all the ordinances; and all the people answered with one voice, and said, "All the words which the Lord has spoken we will do." And Moses wrote all the words of the Lord. And he rose early in the morning, and built an altar at the foot of the mountain, and twelve pillars, according to the twelve tribes of Israel. And he sent young men of the people of Israel, who offered burnt offerings and sacrificed peace offerings of oxen to the Lord. And Moses took half of the blood and put it in basins, and half of the blood he threw against the altar. Then he took the book of the covenant, and read it in the hearing of the people; and they said, "All that the Lord has spoken we will do, and we will be obedient." And Moses took the blood and threw it upon the people, and said, "Behold the blood of the covenant which the Lord has made with you in accordance with all these words."

*Luke 22:15-20*

And he said to them, "I have earnestly desired to eat this passover with you before I suffer; for I tell you I shall not eat it until it is fulfilled in the kingdom of God." And he took a cup, and when he had given thanks he said, "Take this, and divide it among yourselves; for I tell you that from now on I shall not drink of the fruit of the vine until the kingdom of God comes." And he took bread, and when he had given thanks he broke it and gave it to them, saying, "This is my body which is given for you. Do this in remembrance of me." And likewise the cup after supper, saying, "This cup which is poured out for you is the new covenant in my blood."

## Reflection

This is the turning-point of history. First Jesus accomplishes the rites of the old covenant commemorated by the pasch; this was what made Israel a people and gave them that unique relationship to God which forms the backbone of their history as God gradually prepares them for the supreme moment. Both at the eating of the paschal lamb and at the drinking of the cup which finishes off the ceremony Jesus stresses that the kingdom is about to come. He must mean, therefore, that in some way the kingdom comes in the Eucharist which follows, and this is so, for in it is acted out his sacrifice which fulfils the kingdom.

It is possible to concentrate on three moments in the account of the Eucharist. First, it is to be done in memory of him, which gives it the dimension of looking back to his passion and resurrection. Secondly, it is the present sacrifice; it is given and poured out now; in the old covenant the blood was poured out over the altar (representing God) and the people as a bond of unity between them; this bond is even firmer in its almost brutal realism, since the disciples actually drink his blood — and to the Hebrew the blood is the life, so that the disciples take his life into themselves. Thirdly, the dimension of a covenant is open-ended towards the future: it forms a permanent bond between us which has no end, and can only go on getting deeper and deeper, or rather more and more real to us in our lives.

When one takes this passage seriously, that we are really given his body to eat and his blood to drink, it is possible to be almost horrified by the realism of it. The rite takes up the most primitive and elemental ideas of cannibalism, that by so receiving him into ourselves we receive his strength and power. The closest and fullest union which is possible to men is the sexual union, but this is more total even than that, so that in the fullest sense we can become with Christ one flesh, one single thinking, acting unit.

# 5

## THE HELPER

*Isaiah 11:1-2*

There shall come forth a shoot from the stump of Jesse,
    and a branch shall grow out of his roots.
And the Spirit of the Lord shall rest upon him,
    the spirit of wisdom and understanding,
    the spirit of counsel and might,
    the spirit of knowledge and the fear of the Lord.

*John 14:25-27*

These things I have spoken to you, while I am still with
you. But the Counsellor, the Holy Spirit, whom the
Father will send in my name, he will teach you all things,
and bring to your remembrance all that I have said to
you. Peace I leave with you; my peace I give to you;
not as the world gives do I give to you. Let not your
hearts be troubled, neither let them be afraid.

*Romans 8:22-26*

We know that the whole creation has been groaning in
travail together until now; and not only the creation, but
we ourselves, who have the first fruits of the Spirit,
groan inwardly as we wait for adoption as sons, the
redemption of our bodies. For in this hope we were

saved. Now hope that is seen is not hope. For who hopes for what he sees? But if we hope for what we do not see, we wait for it with patience.

Likewise the Spirit helps us in our weakness; for we do not know how to pray as we ought, but the Spirit himself intercedes for us with sighs too deep for words....

## Reflection

The Spirit which Jesus promises is his own Spirit which was prophesied in Isaiah, which was on him as messiah. And it is the realization that we possess this Spirit which makes all the difference to Paul; it gives a totally new aspect to the whole of creation which is struggling to be free and reaching towards its goal like a chick coming out of an egg. And especially to us; for it gives us the extraordinary relationship with the Father of being his adopted sons, so that we can approach him in confidence, knowing that we find in him love, understanding and the strong but firm hand of help. This is surely the secret of the peace which Christ promises at the same time; for if we really believe that we stand in this relationship to the Father we can never lose our peace of mind. It is not a peace such as the world gives; for the problems of the world are such that if one takes them conscientiously peace can only be facile optimism or despairing resigna-tion — unless there is the peace of faith and confidence in the Father. Even so, the peace of Christians is not a flabby satisfaction that God can put everything right if he wants; for this leaves out of account that we too work in the Spirit, and we too 'groan inwardly as we wait for the redemption of our bodies'; the presence in us of the Spirit binds us to share God's interest in his creation, and to work also in its continuing creativity.

The mysteries of the Trinity seem particularly unfathomable in this matter of the Spirit which Jesus promised us. Sometimes it seems that the Paraclete makes Christ present, sometimes that it is the equivalent in his absence. Again, in what way is the Spirit our spirit? How can we say that we are shot through with the Spirit of Christ and of God when we know quite well that we are a long way from living in the spirit of Christ? Be that as it may, it is Christ's bequest of his Spirit which forms the life-principle of the Church and penetrates into each of its furthest members. We might realize the difference it makes by comparing the difference between light and darkness in a room, or between a live animal (or person) and a carcase.

**6**

# THE TRUE VINE

*Isaiah 5:1-7*

Let me sing for my beloved
    a love song concerning his vineyard:

My beloved had a vineyard
    on a very fertile hill.
He digged it and cleared it of stones,
    and planted it with choice vines;
he built a watchtower in the midst of it,
    and hewed out a winevat in it;
and he looked for it to yield grapes
    but it yielded wild grapes.
And now, O inhabitants of Jerusalem
    and men of Judah,
judge, I pray you, between me
    and my vineyard.
What more was there to do for my vineyard,
    that I have not done in it?
When I looked for it to yield grapes,
    why did it yield wild grapes?
And now I will tell you
    what I will do to my vineyard,
I will remove its hedge,
    and it shall be devoured;
I will break down its wall,
    and it shall be trampled down.

I will make it a waste;
    it shall not be pruned or hoed,
    and briers and thorns shall grow up;
I will also command the clouds
    that they rain no rain upon it.
For the vineyard of the Lord of hosts
    is the house of Israel,
and the men of Judah
    are his pleasant planting;
and he looked for justice,
    but behold, bloodshed;
for righteousness,
    but behold, a cry!

*John 15:1-10*

"I am the true vine, and my Father is the vinedresser. Every branch of mine that bears no fruit, he takes away, and every branch that does bear fruit he prunes that it may bear more fruit. You are already made clean by the word which I have spoken to you. Abide in me, and I in you. As the branch cannot bear fruit by itself, unless it abides in the vine, neither can you, unless you abide in me. I am the vine, you are the branches. He who abides in me, and I in him, he it is that bears much fruit, for apart from me you can do nothing. If a man does not abide in me, he is cast forth as a branch and withers; and the branches are gathered, thrown into the fire and burned. If you abide in me, and my words abide in you, ask whatever you will, and it shall be done for you. By this my Father is glorified, that you bear much fruit, and so prove to be my disciples. As the Father has loved me, so have I loved you; abide in my love. If you keep my commandments, you will abide in my love, just as I have kept my Father's commandments and abide in his love."

# Reflection

A vine is not an easy plant to cultivate at the best of times, and especially in the light, stony and unwatered soil of Palestine it needs a great deal of loving attention. So in the Old Testament, as enemy forces began to gather against Judah, Isaiah had taken the vineyard as the symbol of Israel on which God lavished such constant care, to bring home to the chosen people their ingratitude, and threaten them that at last God's patience would come to an end. In the parable of the vine-dressers Our Lord uses the same figure to bring home to the leaders of the people that they are not tending the vineyard as the owner who entrusted it to them had charged them. But in this parable of the vine here Jesus teaches that — to pass from symbol to reality — the true vine which Isaiah envisaged is not Israel at all but is himself.

He is in himself the true people of God, and it is only in so far as we are in him that we are the people of God. So when he undergoes his passion he does it not only for us all, but in the person of us all. Paul puts the other side of the coin when he teaches that by baptism we take on Christ's history as our own, and make our own his death and resurrection, so that his past is now our past and his pulse is now ours. It is hard to see how I can become another person, at least without compromising my own identity, but this is a unique case where all models fail and only analogies can grope for the truth. So many figures are interwoven in the attempt to bring home this vital link between us and Christ: his Spirit is my Spirit, and I am in him as a branch in the vine; his suffering, death and resurrection have by baptism become experiences which I have undergone, and I am a limb of his body.

This is at the same time an immense strength and an immense responsibility. My sufferings and joys receive their fullest worth by being Christ's sufferings and joys, 'filling up the measure' of his own, as Paul tells us. At the same time my actions are perforce his, and I can take Christ's body and make it over to a harlot (1 Cor. 6:15). In the fullest sense my actions and Christ's are one; I am his to the fingertips.

# 7

# THE WORD OF THE FATHER

*Romans 5:15-19*

The free gift is not like the trespass. For if many died through one man's trespass, much more have the grace of God and the free gift in the grace of that one man Jesus Christ abounded for many. And the free gift is not like the effect of that one man's sin. For the judgment following one trespass brought condemnation, but the free gift following many trespasses brings justification. If, because of one man's trespass, death reigned through that one man, much more will those who receive the abundance of grace and the free gift of righteousness reign in life through the one man Jesus Christ.

Then as one man's trespass led to condemnation for all men, so one man's act of righteousness leads to acquittal and life for all men. For as by one man's disobedience many were made sinners, so by one man's obedience many will be made righteous.

*John 17:4-10*

"I glorified thee on earth, having accomplished the work which thou gavest me to do; and now, Father, glorify thou me in thy own presence with the glory which I had with thee before the world was made.

"I have manifested thy name to the men whom thou gavest me out of the world; thine they were, and thou gavest them to me, and they have kept thy word. Now they know that everything that thou hast given me is from thee; for I have given them the words which thou gavest me, and they have received them and know in truth that I came from thee; and they have believed that thou didst send me. I am praying for them; I am not praying for the world but for those whom thou hast given me, for they are thine; all mine are thine, and thine are mine, and I am glorified in them."


## Reflection

In past ages, and a different spirituality, the passion and death of our Lord were sometimes imagined as a scene of retribution or vicarious punishment: God visited on his Son the punishment that was due to us all, and so satiated his fury against the human race. This gives a horrible picture of God, a God of wrath and unforgiving harshness, exacting his pound of flesh, or plunging a knife into the heart of his Son. But, as John shows us here, the reality is quite other: there was no cleft, even temporary, between Father and Son as punisher and punished, but rather the most intimate moment of union. The secret of the passion is not a paroxysm which spent all fury, but a climax of union; for at this moment the obedience of the Son is made perfect, and obedience has sense only as a total union of will and desire.

However it is represented in the story of Adam and Eve in the garden, the fact of man's sin was disobedience to God and assertion of his own independence. Christ's action undoes this, not by carrying out a punishment due for it, but by negating it: as the perfect man, the natural representative of the human race because he is the crown of all creation, Christ submits totally to the

Father. If anyone, he has the right to independence by reason of his position, but yet he is obedient. It is not really a *submission* in obedience; for this still implies some fundamental difference of desires, as though there was a desire which was suppressed for a greater good; here the union is so complete that there is, paradoxically, only joy in that union.

John insists throughout his gospel that Christ's 'hour', the moment of his glorification, is the moment of his passion and resurrection — not of his resurrection alone but of his passion too. The reason for this is surely that already in the passion — as expressed also in Christ's final prayer before he goes to Gethsemane — Christ is exalted by the perfect union of his will in obedience to the Father. The resurrection then has only to declare this exaltation to the world.

# 8

## PROPHECY OF PETER'S DENIAL

*2 Samuel 15:13-23*

A messenger came to David, saying, "The hearts of the men of Israel have gone after Absalom." Then David said to all his servants who were with him at Jerusalem, "Arise, and let us flee; or else there will be no escape for us from Absalom; go in haste, lest he overtake us quickly, and bring down evil upon us, and smite the city with the edge of the sword." And the king's servants said to the king, "Behold, your servants are ready to do whatever my lord the king decides." So the king went forth, and all his household after him. And the king left ten concubines to keep the house. And the king went forth, and all the people after him; and they halted at the last house. And all his servants passed by him; and all the Cherethites, and all the Pelethites, and all the six hundred Gittites who had followed him from Gath, passed on before the king.

Then the king said to Ittai the Gittite, "Why do you also go with us? Go back, and stay with the king; for you are a foreigner, and also an exile from your home. You came only yesterday, and shall I today make you wander about with us, seeing I go I know not where? Go back, and take your brethren with you; and may the Lord show steadfast love and faithfulness to you." But Ittai answered the king, "As the Lord lives, and as my lord the king lives, wherever my lord the king shall be, whether for death or for life, there also will your servant be." And David said to Ittai, "Go then, pass on." So Ittai the Gittite passed on, with all his men and all the little ones who were with him. And all the country wept aloud as all the people passed by, and the king crossed the brook Kidron, and all the people passed on toward the wilderness.

*Mark 14:26-31*

And when they had sung a hymn, they went out to the Mount of Olives. And Jesus said to them, "You will all fall away; for it is written, 'I will strike the shepherd, and the sheep will be scattered.' But after I am raised up, I will go before you to Galilee." Peter said to him, "Even though they all fall away, I will not." And Jesus said to him, "Truly, I say to you, this very night, before the cock crows twice, you will deny me three times." But he said vehemently, "If I must die with you, I will not deny you." And they all said the same.

## Reflection

By little touches of language Peter's promise of undying fidelity to his master is put by the evangelists in contrast with the promises of Ittai of Gath, a foreign mercenary, to his master David. It was at just such a moment, heavy with gloom and threat for the future, that David was about to leave Jerusalem, driven by the rebellion of his son Absalom, and cross the brook Kidron on his way up the Mount of Olives to the east. And Ittai, a Philistine with no ties of race, and only just received into David's service, remained faithful with all his men, while Peter and the rest of the apostles flee. Jesus does not even say that Peter will be faithful till morning, in spite of his protestations; for the cocks in Jerusalem are notoriously unstable, and sometimes seem to crow all the night through, whenever there is such a sound as a dog barking. There would be a shade of dignity if Peter could have been faithful through the night, but Jesus tells him in effect that at the slightest touch or chance he will deny him.

The impetuosity of the leader of the apostles shows itself again and again in the gospels: he jumps out of the boat to walk to Jesus and then loses confidence and begins to sink. He produces the bright idea at the transfiguration of the three arbours, showing that he has got quite the wrong end of the stick (for the two subsidiary figures are there only to witness to Jesus, and anyway it is only a momentary experience). Even after Pentecost he does not seem to have been made perfect, so that the contrast between before and after, to show the power of the Spirit, will not work: in the controversy about relationships between Jewish and gentile Christians Peter seems to have been cowed by some envoys from Jerusalem into deserting his principles, and had to be rebuked by Paul. It was not only Peter: throughout the gospel, especially in Mark (the other gospels try to iron it out), Jesus is constantly drawing attention to their lack of understanding. They do seem to have been pretty slow, a very average collection. But the comfort is that these were the ones whom Jesus chose; he didn't expect us all to be paragons of spiritual perception and shining models of fidelity; he just wanted us to struggle along.

**9**

# THE AGONY

*Genesis 22:1-14*

After these things God tested Abraham, and said to
him, "Abraham!" And he said, "Here am I." He said,
"Take your son, your only son Isaac, whom you love,
and go to the land of Moriah, and offer him there as a
burnt offering upon one of the mountains of which I
shall tell you." So Abraham rose early in the morning,
saddled his ass, and took two of his young men with
him, and his son Isaac; and he cut the wood for the
burnt offering, and arose and went to the place of which
God had told him. On the third day Abraham lifted up
his eyes and saw the place afar off. Then Abraham said
to his young men, "Stay here with the ass; I and the
lad will go yonder and worship, and come again to you."
And Abraham took the wood of the burnt offering, and
laid it on Isaac his son; and he took in his hand the fire
and the knife. So they went both of them together. And
Isaac said to his father Abraham, "My father!" And he
said, "Here am I, my son." He said, "Behold, the fire
and the wood; but where is the lamb for a burnt
offering?" Abraham said, "God will provide himself the
lamb for a burnt offering, my son." So they went both
of them together.

When they came to the place of which God had told
him, Abraham built an altar there, and laid the wood in
order, and bound Isaac his son, and laid him on the

altar, upon the wood. Then Abraham put forth his hand, and took the knife to slay his son. But the angel of the Lord called to him from heaven, and said, "Abraham, Abraham!" And he said, "Here am I." He said, "Do not lay your hand on the lad or do anything to him; for now I know that you fear God, seeing you have not withheld your son, your only son, from me." And Abraham lifted up his eyes and looked, and behold, behind him was a ram, caught in a thicket by his horns; and Abraham went and took the ram, and offered it up as a burnt offering instead of his son. So Abraham called the name of that place The Lord will provide; as it is said to this day, "On the mount of the Lord it shall be provided."

## Mark 14:32-42

And they went to a place which was called Gethsemane; and he said to his disciples, "Sit here, while I pray." And he took with him Peter and James and John, and began to be greatly distressed and troubled. And he said to them, "My soul is very sorrowful, even to death; remain here, and watch." And going a little farther, he fell on the ground and prayed that, if it were possible, the hour might pass from him. And he said, "Abba, Father, all things are possible to thee; remove this cup from me; yet not what I will, but what thou wilt." And he came and found them sleeping, and he said to Peter, "Simon, are you asleep? Could you not watch one hour? Watch and pray that you may not enter into temptation; the spirit indeed is willing, but the flesh is weak." And again he went away and prayed, saying the same words. And again he came and found them sleeping, for their eyes were very heavy; and they did not know what to answer him. And he came the third time, and said to them, "Are you still sleeping and taking your rest? It is enough; the hour has come; the Son of man is betrayed into the hands of sinners. Rise, let us be going; see, my betrayer is at hand."

## Reflection

One is tempted to ask what hope there is for us in our prayers if even the prayer of Jesus was not answered. And yet here we have the perfect prayer and sacrifice, made in complete confidence, as was the sacrifice by Abraham of his son Isaac. Abraham had been called to give up everything, and now in his old age the one hope of his nomadic desert life was his son, and this too he submitted to God; there is some similarity between his offering as he climbed the mountain and that of Jesus on the Mount of Olives. One cannot really say that his prayer was unanswered. It was a prayer instinct with the greatest love; this is brought home by his invocation 'Abba, Father'; for 'Abba' is the intimate word children use to their father; it has all the warmth, simplicity and trust which is contained in the attitude of a child to its father; the fact that Jesus taught his disciples to use this expression to call on God so struck the early Christians that its Aramaic form was retained — as though they could not believe it to be true, and must hang on to the actual word as a guarantee — even in the Greek-speaking Churches.

In the same way as this 'Abba' brings us into the picture by reminding us that Jesus has invited and enabled us to share his position of son to the Father, so we are reminded of our sharing in Jesus' abandonment to the Father's will: Matthew deliberately gives the wording of the second prayer as 'Thy will be done', using the wording of the prayer which Jesus taught Christians to make their own.

The distinction between prayer and sacrifice seems to have become rather dim in the time of Jesus, for

43

prayer could be called a sacrifice of oneself to God. The prayer of the agony was surely the perfect prayer of love and obedience. Jesus was not granted the release for which he asked, but his prayer did not go unanswered. Perhaps when we look for a certain sort of answer to prayer we are looking for the wrong thing.

**10**

# THE ARREST

*2 Kings 1:2-17*

Ahaziah fell through the lattice in his upper chamber in
Samaria, and lay sick; so he sent messengers, telling
them, "Go, inquire of Baalzebub, the god of Ekron,
whether I shall recover from this sickness." But the
angel of the Lord said to Elijah the Tishbite, "Arise, go
up to meet the messengers of the king of Samaria, and
say to them, 'Is it because there is no God in Israel that
you are going to inquire of Baalzebub, the god of Ekron?'
Now therefore thus says the Lord, 'You shall not come
down from the bed to which you have gone, but you
shall surely die.' " So Elijah went.

The messengers returned to the king, and he said to
them, "Why have you returned?" And they said to him,
"There came a man to meet us, and said to us, 'Go back
to the king who sent you, and say to him, Thus says the
Lord, Is it because there is no God in Israel that you
are sending to inquire of Baalzebub, the god of Ekron?
Therefore you shall not come down from the bed to
which you have gone, but shall surely die.' " He said
to them, "What kind of man was he who came to meet
you and told you these things?" They answered him,
"He wore a garment of haircloth, with a girdle of leather
about his loins." And he said, "It is Elijah the Tishbite."

Then the king sent to him a captain of fifty men
with his fifty. He went up to Elijah, who was sitting on

the top of a hill, and said to him, "O man of God, the king says, 'Come down.'" But Elijah answered the captain of fifty, "If I am a man of God, let fire come down from heaven and consume you and your fifty." Then fire came down from heaven, and consumed him and his fifty.

Again the king sent to him another captain of fifty men with his fifty. And he went up and said him, "O man of God, this is the king's order, 'Come down quickly!'" But Elijah answered them, "I I am a man of God, let fire come down from heaven and consume you and your fifty." Then the fire of God came down from heaven and consumed him and his fifty.

Again the king sent the captain of a third fifty with his fifty. And the third captain of fifty went up, and came and fell on his knees before Elijah, and entreated him, "O man of God, I pray you, let my life, and the life of these fifty servants of yours, be precious in your sight. Lo, fire came down from heaven, and consumed the two former captains of fifty men with their fifties; but now let my life be precious in your sight." Then the angel of the Lord said to Elijah, "Go down with him; do not be afraid of him." So he arose and went down with him to the king, and said to him, "Thus says the Lord, 'Because you have sent messengers to inquire of Baalzebub, the god of Ekron, — is it because there is no God in Israel to inquire of his word? — therefore you shall not come down from the bed to which you have gone, but you shall surely die.'"

So he died according to the word of the Lord which Elijah had spoken.


*John 18:1-11*

When Jesus had spoken these words, he went forth with his disciples across the Kidron valley, where there was a garden, which he and his disciples entered. Now Judas, who betrayed him, also knew the place; for Jesus often met there with his disciples. So Judas, procuring a band of soldiers and some officers from the chief priests and the Pharisees, went there with lanterns and torches and weapons. Then Jesus, knowing all that was to befall him, came forward and said to them, "Whom do you seek?" They answered him, "Jesus of Nazareth." Jesus said to them, "I am he." Judas, who betrayed him, was standing with them. When he said to them, "I am he," they drew back and fell to the ground. Again he asked them, "Whom do you seek?" And they said, "Jesus of Nazareth." Jesus answered, "I told you that I am he; so, if you seek me, let these men go." This was to fulfil the word which he had spoken, "Of those whom thou gavest me I lost not one." Then Simon Peter, having a sword, drew it and struck the high priest's slave and cut off his right ear. The slave's name was Malchus. Jesus said to Peter, "Put your sword into its sheath; shall I not drink the cup which the Father has given me?"

## Reflection

In the story of the arrest of Jesus as told by John a theme is clearly visible which will reappear often in John's passion account, and which makes it reminiscent of the Old Testament story of the attempt to arrest Elijah: it is really Jesus who controls the progress of events. Jesus, the victim, is the commanding figure in this scene. They fall back before him overawed as before a supernatural apparition, and indeed he replies with the words which God spoke to Moses, 'I am' (translated 'I am he', but the Greek in which the gospel was written is the same). One is given the impression that it is only when he is ready and has given his consent that they can take him at all. This is part of John's presentation of the passion as the 'hour' of Christ's glorification and exaltation; not merely at his resurrection does he receive his position of full glory as the Word of God made man, but already now, in the course of his humiliation, this shines through. It is also the means of underlining Jesus' willing acceptance of his Father's will. Contrast his majestic control of the situation with Peter's muddled but well-meaning attempt to interfere: Peter flails away with a sword to no purpose, while Jesus by his command alone secures the immunity of the disciples.

The treachery of Judas must have consisted in revealing the place where Jesus would be spending the night; this is less clear in the other gospels than in John; for in the other gospels he spends the last week openly in Jerusalem, whereas according to John the Jews had been looking for an opportunity to kill him since the raising of Lazarus. The traitor's kiss is an unadulterated sham, the greeting of a disciple to his rabbi; by which Judas seeks to explain his presence. The varieties of self-deception which we practise on Christ are immense too; sometimes we seem to do him an act of service when we know quite well that our particular motive is quite other; sometimes we can almost manage to deceive ourselves about our true motives until we look him straight in the face.

**11**

## BEFORE THE SANHEDRIN

*Daniel 7:9-10, 13-14*

As I looked,
    thrones were placed and one that was ancient of days
        took his seat;
his raiment was white as snow,
    and the hair of his head like pure wool;
his throne was fiery flames,
    its wheels were burning fire.
A stream of fire issued
    and came forth from before him;
a thousand thousands served him,
    and ten thousand times ten thousand stood before him;
the court sat in judgment,
    and the books were opened....
I saw in the night visions,
and behold, with the clouds of heaven
    there came one like a son of man,
and he came to the Ancient of Days
    and was presented before him.
And to him was given dominion
    and glory and kingdom,
that all peoples, nations, and languages
    should serve him;
his dominion is an everlasting dominion,
    which shall not pass away,
and his kingdom one
    that shall not be destroyed.

The chief priests and the whole council sought testimony against Jesus to put him to death; but they found none. For many bore false witness against him, and their witness did not agree. And some stood up and bore false witness against him, saying, "We heard him say, 'I will destroy this temple that is made with hands, and in three days I will build another, not made with hands.'" Yet not even so did their testimony agree. And the high priest stood up in the midst, and asked Jesus, "Have you no answer to make? What is it that these men testify against you?" But he was silent and made no answer. Again the high priest asked him, "Are you the Christ, the Son of the Blessed?" And Jesus said, "I am; and you will see the Son of man sitting at the right hand of Power, and coming with the clouds of heaven." And the high priest tore his mantle, and said, "Why do we still need witnesses? You have heard his blasphemy. What is your decision?" And they all condemned him as deserving death.

## Reflection

The accounts of Jesus' interrogation by his Jewish captors are confused and contradictory in the gospels, so that it is difficult to know which is correct, whether there was really a full meeting of the Sanhedrin, hurriedly summoned at dead of night, and a sort of trial, or whether there was simply an interrogation by the high priest during the night, followed by a short confirmatory session of the Sanhedrin in the morning. Whichever is the case, Mark's account shows us the real reason why Jesus was rejected by the Jewish authorities. The first, so most important, accusation was that he spoke against the temple; the witnesses here are said to be false: what he really said was 'If you destroy this temple . . .' or just

'*Destroy* this temple and . . .' (John 2: 19). This remark was regarded, together with the cleansing of the temple, as the limit of reforming zeal which the Sadducees were just not prepared to stomach; it amounted to turning upside-down all their ideas about the immutable sacredness of their elaborate cult system. The second charge was more subtle (it was not a false accusation; for Jesus made the claim himself): the charge relayed to Pilate was that of claiming to be king of the Jews, and so a political revolutionary. But Jesus refers only to Daniel's prophecy that a figure 'like a son of man' would free God's people, and he claims to be that figure, at last making clear the mysterious title which he had used for himself during his ministry; the sharp point of this claim is that Jesus claims before his interrogators to have received from the 'one that was ancient of days' sovereignty over all peoples, a sovereignty which will never pass away, and this they will not accept. So in the end both charges boil down to the same, the claim to have divine authority over all that the Jews held sacred.

It is easy to apply this superficially to ourselves, and ask whether Jesus would receive the same outraged condemnation from the Church (and especially the clergy) today, were he to appear and try to reverse our comfortably accepted way of doing things; a reformer, and especially one who sees too clearly and asks too penetrating questions, is an awkward person to get along with. More searching and relevant still: Jesus is constantly appearing in our lives with his supreme authority, and asking things which go beyond what he ought to ask, unsettling us with outrageous demands which go beyond the life we contracted for. But that was what the Jewish authorities refused to accept.

**12**

# MOCKERY AS A PROPHET

*Isaiah 50:4-9*

The Lord God has given me
    the tongue of those who are taught,
that I may know how to sustain with a word
    him that is weary.
Morning by morning he wakens,
    he wakens my ear to hear as those who are taught.
The Lord God has opened my ear,
    and I was not rebellious,
    I turned not backward.
I gave my back to the smiters,
    and my cheeks to those who pulled out the beard;
I hid not my face
    from shame and spitting.
For the Lord God helps me;
    therefore I have not been confounded;
therefore I have set my face like a flint,
    and I know that I shall not be put to shame;
he who vindicates me is near.
Who will contend with me?
    Let us stand up together.
Who is my adversary?
    Let him come near to me.
Behold, the Lord God helps me;
    who will declare me guilty?
Behold, all of them will wear out like a garment;
    the moth will eat them up.

Then they spat in his face, and struck him; and some slapped him, saying, "Prophesy to us, you Christ! Who is it that struck you?"

## Reflection

Jesus claimed to be a prophet, that is a spokesman with a direct mandate from God to break through the normal institutional channels and declare his will. He must, then, receive knowledge through abnormal channels. So they blindfolded him and mocked his claim to be a prophet by asking him to say who hit him. In Matthew's account the blindfolding, specifically mentioned by Mark and Luke, has dropped out; but instead, by slight retouches, Matthew reminds the reader of the prophecy of Isaiah concerning the Servant of the Lord. Especially for the converts from Judaism for whom Matthew was writing, the shameful humiliation of the Lord was a scandal; he should have come as a glorious figure, all-powerful, all-conquering and acknowledged by all, and as it was he was exposed to insult and mockery. So Matthew, most of all the evangelists, sets out to show by reference to the Old Testament that all this was decreed by the word of God in the scriptures. Different people will assess differently the shame and the physical suffering which the Lord underwent; to one the shame may be more daunting, to another the pain.

It is curious that of recent years it is the Jews who have been subjected to both these more than any other occidentals. When one meets a man who still bears on his arm the brand-mark of the concentration camp it is easy to see how suffering gives depth; for those who have survived this experience are almost always people of great understanding, depth and sympathy. The Letter to the Hebrews (5 : 8-9) speaks of Christ as having been made perfect through suffering; to the perfect man the horror and the enrichment of personality must alike have been immeasurably greater than in any other case.

**13**

## PETER'S DENIAL

*Luke 22:55-62*

When they had kindled a fire in the middle of the
courtyard and sat down together, Peter sat among them.
Then a maid, seeing him as he sat in the light and
gazing at him, said, "This man also was with him." But
he denied it, saying, "Woman, I do not know him." And
a little later some one else saw him and said, "You also
are one of them." But Peter said, "Man, I am not." And
after an interval of about an hour still another insisted,
saying, "Certainly this man also was with him; for he is
a Galilean." But Peter said, "Man, I do not know what
you are saying." And immediately, while he was still
speaking, the cock crowed. And the Lord turned and
looked at Peter. And Peter remembered the word of the
Lord, how he had said to him, "Before the cock crows
today, you will deny me three times." And he went out
and wept bitterly.

*John 21:51-17*

When they had finished breakfast, Jesus said to Simon
Peter, "Simon, son of John, do you love me more than
these?" He said to him, "Yes, Lord; you know that I
love you." He said to him, "Feed my lambs." A second
time he said to him, "Simon, son of John, do you love

me?" He said to him, "Yes, Lord; you know that I love you." He said to him, "Tend my sheep." He said to him the third time, "Simon, son of John, do you love me?" Peter was grieved because he said to him the third time, "Do you love me?" And he said to him, "Lord, you know everything; you know that I love you." Jesus said to him, "Feed my sheep."

## Reflection

The denial takes place with almost casual ease, a mere slip of a girl happens to look at Peter and make a remark, not even necessarily hostile. One can weave such a web of the state Peter must have got himself into to allow himself to do it! 'It hardly matters what I say to someone like that', or 'he has no right to ask', or 'I'll be as non-committal as possible'. And then once he has told one lie he has to sink in deeper and deeper, as is the manner with lying, when one lie so often leads on to another as explanation or confirmation, and what begins with a harmless fib ends with a deliberate lie. Peter's impulsiveness carried him into deep waters. It is Luke alone who puts in the little touch that the Lord turned and looked at Peter. Luke, the first Church historian, is always interested in the phenomenon of conversion, as we shall see also with the good thief, and he is telling us that conversion and, in this case, repentance, start with a glance of the Lord; unless he looks at us there is no hope. There must indeed have been an exchange of looks between the Lord and Peter, which brings him back to his sense of reality; the self-blinding process which alone makes sin possible is dissolved like the morning dew when one can bring oneself to look at Christ.

It is surely to this scene that the triple question of the risen Christ by the lake refers: to the triple denial corresponds the triple profession. There are three separate occasions in the different gospels where Jesus entrusts Peter with his office of leader in the Church, and each is tied to a declaration by Peter. The first is in Matthew at Caesarea Philippi, where Peter proclaims his faith in Jesus as the Christ, the Son of the living God; Jesus replies with the promise that Peter will be the rock on which the Church is built. The last is the passage in John when Peter declares his love and is told to be shepherd of the flock. Between them come the scene at the supper where Peter declares his readiness to die for his Master (Luke 22:31-34); corresponding to this declaration of intention there is only the restrained promise that he will sometime be converted and strengthen his brethren. So Jesus has no illusions about even the chief of his followers; he accepts fully the declaration of faith and of love, but when it comes to the promise of undying fidelity he knows how much this is worth. It is not for nothing that the gospels return so often to the subject of repentance; one might almost call it the chief of the Christian virtues.

# 14

# DEATH OF JUDAS

*2 Samuel 17:1-16, 23*

Ahithophel said to Absalom, "Let me choose twelve thousand men, and I will set out and pursue David tonight. I will come upon him while he is weary and discouraged, and throw him into a panic; and all the people who are with him will flee. I will strike down the king only, and I will bring all the people back to you as a bride comes home to her husband. You seek the life of only one man, and all the people will be at peace." And the advice pleased Absalom and all the elders of Israel.

Then Absalom said, "Call Hushai the Archite also, and let us hear what he has to say." And when Hushai came to Absalom, Absalom said to him, "Thus has Ahithophel spoken; shall we do as he advises? If not, you speak." Then Hushai said to Absalom, "This time the counsel which Ahithophel has given is not good." Hushai said moreover, "You know that your father and his men are mighty men, and that they are enraged, like a bear robbed of her cubs in the field. Besides, your father is expert in war; he will not spend the night with the people. Behold, even now he has hidden himself in one of the pits, or in some other place. And when some of the people fall at the first attack, whoever hears it will say, 'There has been a slaughter among the people who follow Absalom.' Then even the valiant man, whose heart is like the heart of a lion, will utterly melt with fear; for all Israel knows that your father is a mighty man, and that those who are with him are valiant men. But my counsel is that all Israel be gathered to you, from Dan to Beer-sheba, as the sand by the sea for multitude, and that you go to battle in person. So we shall come upon him in some place where he is to be found, and we shall light upon him as the dew falls on the ground; and of him and all the men with him not one will be left. If he withdraws into a city, then all Israel will bring ropes to that city, and we shall drag it into the valley, until not even a pebble is to be found there." And Absalom and all the men of Israel said, "The counsel of Hushai the Archite is better than the counsel of Ahithophel." For the Lord had ordained to defeat the good counsel of Ahithophel, so that the Lord might bring evil upon Absalom.

Then Hushai said to Zadok and Abiathar the priests, "Thus and so did Ahithophel counsel Absalom and the elders of Israel; and thus and so have I counselled. Now therefore send quickly and tell David, 'Do not lodge tonight at the fords of the wilderness, but by all means pass over; lest the king and all the people who are with him be swallowed up.' ". . . .

When Ahithophel saw that his counsel was not followed, he saddled his ass, and went off home to his own city. And he set his house in order, and hanged himself; and he died, and was buried in the tomb of his father.


*Matthew 27:3-10*

When Judas, his betrayer, saw that he was condemned, he repented and brought back the thirty pieces of silver to the chief priests and the elders, saying, "I have sinned in betraying innocent blood." They said, "What is that to us? See to it yourself." And throwing down the pieces of silver in the temple, he departed; and he went and hanged himself. But the chief priests, taking the pieces of silver, said, "It is not lawful to put them into the treasury, since they are blood money." So they took counsel, and bought with them the potter's field, to bury strangers in. Therefore that field has been called the Field of Blood to this day. Then was fulfilled what had been spoken by the prophet Jeremiah, saying, "And they took the thirty pieces of silver, the price of him on whom a price had been set by some of the sons of Israel, and they gave them for the potter's field, as the Lord directed me."

## Reflection

As in the episode of Peter's promise never to desert his Master, the gospel again draws attention to the parallel between Jesus and David, but this time especially to Ahithophel who had been David's faithful counsellor but deserted him and betrayed him to Absalom. We may infer from the different account of Judas' death in Acts 1: 18-19 (where there are other scriptural allusions to a traitor's death) that Matthew is less describing what actually happened than drawing attention to the fate of the traitor who betrays his Master.

Traditionally Judas is damned out of hand, with a glance at the saying 'Better for that man had he never been born' which, taken literally, can mean only this. But it does seem merciless to rate his repentance so low. He did, after all, get as far as acknowledging that he had sinned, even though the desperation caused by the horror of realization of his sin led him, according to Matthew's account, to the extreme of suicide. However, as Acts does not make this clear, it may be that Matthew is adopting from the Old Testament parallel the description of the classic death of a traitor, to fill a gap where he has no information. Anyway Judas was clearly in a frenzy of grief and guilt. And the saying of Jesus can hardly be taken as a condemnation to all eternity; it seeks to show the enormity of the crime rather than the inability of the sinner to repent. It is another of those virile Palestinian sayings of the Lord like the one about hating father and mother, which it is dangerous to take with a pedestrian literalness. Perhaps one should not whitewash Judas too thoroughly, but it is attractive to see him as a type of repentance; wild and misguided though the course of action here described is, it is only a witness to the depth of his repentance.

What about hell anyway? If Judas isn't there, who is? But whether anyone is in it or not, the state of total aversion from God is useful to conceive. The idea of having turned one's back resolutely and finally on God conjures up a darkness, cold and joyless grimness which does help to freshen up by contrast the light, joy and vitality of his creative presence.

**15**

# BEFORE PILATE

*Psalm 99:1-5*

The Lord reigns; let the peoples tremble!
He sits enthroned upon the cherubim; let the earth quake!
The Lord is great in Zion;
    he is exalted over all the peoples.
Let them praise thy great and terrible name!
    Holy is he!
Mighty King, lover of justice,
    thou hast established equity;
thou hast executed justice
    and righteousness in Jacob.
Extol the Lord our God;
    worship at his footstool!
    Holy is he!

*John 18:28—19:15*

Then they led Jesus from the house of Caiaphas to the
praetorium. It was early. They themselves did not enter
the praetorium, so that they might not be defiled, but
might eat the passover. So Pilate went out to them and
said, "What accusation do you bring against this man?"
They answered him, "If this man were not an evildoer,
we would not have handed him over." Pilate said to
them, "Take him yourselves and judge him by your

own law." The Jews said to him, "It is not lawful for us to put any man to death." This was to fulfil the word which Jesus had spoken to show by what death he was to die.

Pilate entered the practorium again and called Jesus, and said to him, "Are you the King of the Jews?" Jesus answered, "Do you say this of your own accord, or did others say it to you about me?" Pilate answered, "Am I a Jew? Your own nation and the chief priests have handed you over to me; what have you done?" Jesus answered, "My kingship is not of this world; if my kingship were of this world, my servants would fight, that I might not be handed over to the Jews; but my kingship is not from the world." Pilate said to him, "So you are a king?" Jesus answered, "You say that I am a king. For this I was born, and for this I have come into the world, to bear witness to the truth. Every one who is of the truth hears my voice." Pilate said to him, "What is truth?"

After he had said this, he went out to the Jews again, and told them, "I find no crime in him. But you have a custom that I should release one man for you at the Passover; will you have me release for you the King of the Jews?" They cried out again, "Not this man, but Barabbas!" Now Barabbas was a robber.

Then Pilate took Jesus and scourged him. And the soldiers plaited a crown of thorns, and put it on his head, and arrayed him in a purple robe; they came up to him, saying, "Hail, King of the Jews!" and struck him with their hands. Pilate went out again, and said to them, "Behold, I am bringing him out to you, that you may know that I find no crime in him." So Jesus came out, wearing the crown of thorns and the purple robe. Pilate said to them, "Here is the man!" When the chief priests and the officers saw him, they cried out, "Crucify him, crucify him!" Pilate said to them, "Take him yourselves and crucify him, for I find no crime in him." The Jews answered him, "We have a law, and by that law he ought to die, because he has made himself the Son of God." When Pilate heard these words, he was the more afraid; he entered the praetorium again and said to Jesus, "Where are you from?" But Jesus gave no answer. Pilate therefore said to him, "You will not speak to me? Do you not know that I have power to release you, and power to crucify you?" Jesus answered him, "You would have no power over me unless it had been given you from above; therefore he who delivered me to you has the greater sin."

Upon this Pilate sought to release him, but the Jews cried out, "If you release this man, you are not Caesar's friend; every one who makes himself a king sets himself against Caesar." When Pilate heard these words, he brought Jesus out and sat down on the judgment seat at a place called The Pavement, and in Hebrew, Gabbatha. Now it was the day of Preparation of the Passover; it was about the sixth hour. He said to the Jews, "Here is your King!" They cried out, "Away with him, away with him, crucify him!" Pilate said to them, "Shall I crucify your King?" The chief priests answered, "We have no king but Caesar."

## Reflection

The account of this trial scene (if one can call it a trial — it is rather Pilate's refusal to try Jesus) given by John is more elaborate than that of the other evangelists. One might say it was a carefully constructed tragedy, where scenes inside the praetorium and outside it alternate exactly and where the scenes correspond, the first to the last, the second to the penultimate, and so on. The centre-piece is therefore the scene where Jesus is crowned king by the soldiers, and another climax occurs at the end where the Jews deny any kingship but that of Caesar. The tragedy comes in the contrast: in the Old Testament, and especially in the temple liturgy, the theme of the kingship of Yahweh becomes more and more important as time progresses; it is preparing for the full manifestation of this kingship with the coming of the messiah. The preparation for and the welcoming of the messiah was the whole reason for the existence of the chosen people. And now at the moment of his manifestation they deny him, and not only him but Yahweh's kingship too, 'we have no king but Caesar'. At the same time John sees Jesus' kingship to be acknowledged by the heathen soldiers, who mock him for it but do not deny it.

Here, then, is the climax of the gospel. All the way through there has been a series of confrontations with Jesus, and men are judged by their reaction to him. To be more exact, they judge themselves by whether they welcome the light or shun it, whether they come to the light or cannot face it. As John makes clear, it is a process which continues throughout history in the confrontation with Christ: we are judged, or are pronouncing our own sentence, by our reaction to Christ. These confrontations with him occur daily, not only in 'religious' spheres such as prayer, but in every meeting where there is a demand made on us or an opportunity opened for us. Especially in an encounter with a person, where we have the choice of recognizing Christ in him, as the Jews had the opportunity of recognizing the messiah-king in Jesus, are we pronouncing the sentence. And we are in the same position as the Jews, long prepared for this moment. One constantly has ground to be thankful that the denials of Christ's kingship made in missing opportunities, and the self-judgment of turning from the light, are not so total and final.

# 16

# BEFORE HEROD

*1 Corinthians 1:18-25*

For the word of the cross is folly to those who are
perishing, but to us who are being saved it is the power
of God. For it is written,

"I will destroy the wisdom of the wise, and the
cleverness of the clever I will thwart."

Where is the wise man? Where is the scribe? Where
is the debater of this age? Has not God made foolish the
wisdom of the world? For since, in the wisdom of God,
the world did not know God through wisdom, it pleased
God through the folly of what we preach to save those
who believe. For Jews demand signs and Greeks seek
wisdom, but we preach Christ crucified, a stumbling
block to Jews and folly to Gentiles, but to those who
are called, both Jews and Greeks, Christ the power of
God and the wisdom of God. For the foolishness of
God is wiser than men, and the weakness of God is
stronger than men.

*Luke 23:6-12*

When Pilate heard this, he asked whether the man was a
Galilean. And when he learned that he belonged to
Herod's jurisdiction, he sent him over to Herod, who

was himself in Jerusalem at that time. When Herod saw Jesus, he was very glad, for he had long desired to see him, because he had heard about him, and he was hoping to see some sign done by him. So he questioned him at some length; but he made no answer. The chief priests and the scribes stood by, vehemently accusing him. And Herod with his soldiers treated him with contempt and mocked him; then, arraying him in gorgeous apparel, he sent him back to Pilate. And Herod and Pilate became friends with each other that very day, for before this they had been at enmity with each other.

## Reflection

Luke makes much of this meeting with Herod, the Jewish ruler of Galilee, though it is not mentioned by the other evangelists, because for him Herod is the type of Jewish disbelief. Herod wants to see a glittering display from Jesus, either miracles like conjuring tricks or at least eloquence; he is half Jew and half Greek — mostly Jewish by blood, but hellenized by education — so that he aptly falls under both halves of Paul's stricture, 'Jews demand signs and Greeks seek wisdom'. The signs he wanted are presumably marvels such as occur in profusion in contemporary Jewish literature, (whether they actually happened is more questionable), like streams flowing uphill or trees uprooting from one place to another. But the signs of God which Jesus offers are less spectacular and more realistic, less superficial and more profound, which is why the power of God and the wisdom of God can be a stumbling-block so easily. The values of Christ do not necessarily spring to the eye, and it may take time and patience to discern them in a person or a situation. But Herod was not prepared to listen profoundly and open himself to Christ's message; he just wanted the thrill. There is a good deal of analogy here to our own case: we do not learn all about Christ in a flash but can always penetrate deeper into his mystery and into its meaning in our lives. To live as a Christian is not glamorous and sparkling; the light of the cross is more subdued and needs more patience and tranquillity to be seen.

There are two other little ideas in this passage which add something. The first is one which is never far from Luke's thoughts: the Christian must follow his master in bearing witness under persecution. Jesus had said that in persecution his disciples would be dragged before sanhedrins, governors and kings for the sake of his name; just so Paul, in the Acts of the Apostles, will have to make his defence and bear his witness before all these bodies, ending with Herod Agrippa, the successor of the Herod before whom Jesus now stands. Jesus goes before in the suffering which his followers must undergo. The other idea which Luke notes is that even at this moment Jesus brings peace and reconciliation: Pilate and Herod had been at variance for some time, but now they are brought together through Jesus.

**17**

# THE SENTENCE

*Deuteronomy 21:6-9*

And all the elders of that city nearest to the slain man shall wash their hands over the heifer whose neck was broken in the valley; and they shall testify, 'Our hands did not shed this blood, neither did our eyes see it shed. Forgive, O Lord, thy people Israel, whom thou hast redeemed, and set not the guilt of innocent blood in the midst of thy people Israel; but let the guilt of blood be forgiven them.' So you shall purge the guilt of innocent blood from your midst.

*Matthew 27:24-26*

So when Pilate saw that he was gaining nothing, but rather that a riot was beginning, he took water and washed his hands before the crowd, saying, "I am innocent of this righteous man's blood; see to it yourselves." And all the people answered, "His blood be on us and on our children!" Then he released for them Barabbas, and having scourged Jesus, delivered him to be crucified.

## Reflection

To make it abundantly clear where the responsibility lies for Jesus' death Matthew includes the little scene of Pilate washing his hands. It is only ironical that the gesture which was prescribed by the Law to symbolize the removal of guilt from the people of Israel should here symbolize precisely the clearance of the gentile Pilate at the expense of the chosen people.

It is this scene which has captured the Christian imagination, and been used down the ages to justify so much harshness to and persecution of the Jews. But Paul is far gentler; in his letter to the Romans he tells of his anguish at their failure to respond. He does not condemn them but longs with his whole being for their salvation. In his imaginary dialogue there with non-Jewish Christians, as soon as there is an opening for condemnation he rounds on the gentile and points to the mystery of God's free choice: God chooses whom he will, and those whom he chooses cannot vaunt themselves on being chosen. Continually through history there was a process of selection going on, again and again a remnant chosen, and the others left. Why, then, was I chosen? First of all I was chosen, from all possible combinations and varieties of faults and qualities, to exist; in his impenetrable will God decided that it should be me. And then, from all the countless myriads of human beings who have existed and will exist he chose such a small number to receive the light of the gospel and included me.

But what should I do? Again to the Romans Paul writes that the Jews could not achieve salvation by obedience to the law. It is almost impossible to visualize the fidelity and devotion which this obedience to the law involved, a constriction and servitude which reached into every aspect of daily living, so that for the faithful Jew the law was really constantly before his eyes to a greater extent perhaps even than Christian practices prescribe the details of daily living for a modern religious or priest. And yet to no avail. Such a large proportion of the gospel consists in overturning all this for the freedom of Christ. All that Paul requires is faith, the faith of Abraham, which means total dedication and trust in the Lord. One can never win salvation, only open oneself to receive it. Yet the danger of trying to do so, just as the Jews tried, is still with us.

**18**

# THE ROAD TO CALVARY

*Mark 8:34-37*

He called to him the multitude with his disciples, and said to them, "If any man would come after me, let him deny himself and take up his cross and follow me. For whoever would save his life will lose it; and whoever loses his life for my sake and the gospel's will save it. For what does it profit a man, to gain the whole world and forfeit his life? For what can a man give in return for his life?"

*Luke 23:26*

As they led him away, they seized one Simon of Cyrene, who was coming in from the country, and laid on him the cross, to carry it behind Jesus.

*John 19:17*

... and he went out, bearing his own cross, to the place called the place of a skull, which is called in Hebrew Golgotha.

# Reflection

Normally a prisoner on his way out to execution carried the transverse arm of the cross, as the upright remained permanently fixed in the ground. According to Mark, Simon of Cyrene carried Jesus' for him — perhaps he was too exhausted to do so himself — and Luke adds that Simon carried it 'behind' Jesus, indicating that he is fulfilling the instructions for a follower of Jesus. This carrying of the instrument of execution was the final humiliation, as the condemned would carry it through the crowded streets of the town as an example to others. Normally he was already stripped, but this does not seem to have been the case with Jesus; for the hellenistic world the Jews were unusually touchy in such matters. The object was, however, to expose the condemned to as much ridicule and insult as possible — in all of which no doubt Simon had his share as the first to carry the cross behind Jesus.

Nevertheless John's description suggests the triumphant bearing of a banner of victory. He always looks at the crucifixion with the eyes of faith: it is the means by which Jesus achieves his glory, and John's vision of it is so suffused already with the light of its goal that the suffering and humiliation pale beside this. For centuries in the Church the cross was always a symbol of triumph and honour, splendid with jewels; it was only when the new devotion to the humanity of our Lord arose in the late middle ages that there was any desire for a realistic representation; till then it was a standard of victory. It was the same spirit of devotion to the suffering humanity of Christ that gave rise to many of the traditions about the way of the cross, such as the three falls or Veronica or the meeting with Mary. None of these occur in the gospels but are simply evidence of the warmth of devotion which led Christians to dwell on and elaborate on the bare narrative of the gospels.

It is possible to combine the two aspects of the cross, and helpful to do so: when we are carrying the cross behind Jesus, dreary and frustrating though this may seem, it is his symbol of triumph that we are bearing.

# 19

# THE WOMEN OF JERUSALEM

*Zechariah 12:10-11; 13:1*

I will pour out on the house of David and the inhabitants of Jerusalem a spirit of compassion and supplication so that, when they look on him whom they have pierced, they shall mourn for him, as one mourns for an only child, and weep bitterly over him as one weeps over a first-born. On that day the mourning in Jerusalem will be as great as the mourning for Hadadrimmon in the plain of Magiddo. . .

On that day there shall be a fountain opened for the house of David and the inhabitants of Jerusalem to cleanse them from sin and uncleanness.

*Luke 23:27-31*

A great multitude of the people followed him, and of women who bewailed and lamented him. But Jesus turning to them said, "Daughters of Jerusalem, do not weep for me, but weep for yourselves and for your children. For behold, the days are coming when they will say, 'Blessed are the barren, and the wombs that never bore, and the breasts that never gave suck!' Then they will begin to say to the mountains, 'Fall on us';

and to the hills, 'Cover us.' For if they do this when the wood is green, what will happen when it is dry?"

*Matthew 27:33-34*

When they came to a place called Golgotha (which means the place of a skull), they offered him wine to drink, mingled with gall; but when he tasted it, he would not drink it.

## Reflection

It appears that there was in Jerusalem at this time a society of charitable women who succoured condemned prisoners on their way to execution, especially by offering them drugged wine as a sort of narcotic to lessen consciousness of their agony. Luke interprets these ministrations and the crowd that followed in function of the prophecy of Zechariah, and sees in them part of the phenomena which would occur at the time of the eschatological victory of Yahweh. The general tone of the passage in Zechariah is different; for it describes a military victory with the destruction of all the nations that oppose Jerusalem; but the prophet is there using warlike imagery to describe the reality of victory which is about to take place on the cross, the destruction of the forces which oppose God's plans and his chosen people. At the same time Jesus gives the warning that there will be no eschatological triumph of Jerusalem, but rather its destruction is already threatening; the victory will not be as Zechariah might lead them to expect.

Luke especially takes an interest in the women who follow Jesus; he is often careful to mention their presence when none of the other evangelists do; it is he who mentions Mary Magdalen, the woman who was a sinner and moistened Jesus' feet with her tears; he alone has the story of Martha and Mary. At the same time he is the evangelist who most often mentions celibacy. From this passage one might start a theology of virginity: the reason why those who have never borne children will be blessed when the final tribulation comes is that they will not mourn their loss, and will not have put all their hope in their children. Thus the denial of having children can be a witness to the fact that one is looking forward to the end, putting all trust and hope in God.

Matthew is reminded by the drugged wine of the psalm 'They gave me poison for food, and for my thirst they gave me vinegar to drink'. From both these Old Testament references one can get an impression of the evangelists' view of these happenings: they are the fulfilment of the long history of the chosen people, when God at last fulfils his age-old promises and brings history to its accomplishment, the moment when all the longing of the ages is satisfied. But to these women their action did not seem so dramatic, probably quite routine, as routine and unglamorous as any small act of kindness done to Christ in his brethren; yet this can be just as momentous.

# 20

# FORGIVENESS

*Acts 7:55-60*

But Stephen, full of the Holy Spirit, gazed into heaven and saw the glory of God, and Jesus standing at the right hand of God; and he said, "Behold, I see the heavens opened, and the Son of man standing at the right hand of God." But they cried out with a loud voice and stopped their ears and rushed together upon him. Then they cast him out of the city and stoned him; and the witnesses laid down their garments at the feet of a young man named Saul. And as they were stoning Stephen, he prayed, "Lord Jesus, receive my spirit." And he knelt down and cried with a loud voice, "Lord, do not hold this sin against them." And when he had said this, he fell asleep.

*Luke 23:33-34, 39-43*

When they came to the place which is called The Skull, there they crucified him, and the criminals, one on the right and one on the left. And Jesus said, "Father, forgive them; for they know not what they do." And they cast lots to divide his garments. . . .

One of the criminals who were hanged railed at him, saying, "Are you not the Christ? Save yourself and us!"

But the other rebuked him, saying, "Do you not fear God, since you are under the same sentence of condemnation? And we indeed justly; for we are receiving the due reward of our deeds; but this man has done nothing wrong." And he said, "Jesus, remember me when you come in your kingly power." And he said to him, "Truly, I say to you, today you will be with me in Paradise."

## Reflection

All through his gospel Luke has shown us a Jesus always ready to forgive and welcome sinners, like Zacchaeus and the woman who was a sinner; his parables are full of the same theme, the lost sheep and the lost coin, and the prodigal son. This is one of the chief messages he must get across, that no matter how great or how frequent a sin, the Lord is always eager to welcome back the sinner at the slightest sign. And so even now, or perhaps especially now, at the climax of the crucifixion Luke records these two scenes, which do not appear in the other evangelists, showing Jesus pardoning sinners. Perhaps by these two scenes of individual forgiveness he is underlining the meaning of the crucifixion as such, the forgiveness of all sin.

In the first scene there are two things which are remarkable, first that the executioners are not repentant, just acting in ignorance. But just how ignorant were they, either in this case or in that of Stephen? It seems almost as though the Lord is clutching at a straw here, especially because in Luke and John it looks as though the execution is carried out not by Romans but by Jews; they must have had some idea of what they were doing, but Jesus is so eager to obtain for them forgiveness that he concentrates on the fact that they did not realize the full extent of their deed. The second remarkable thing is the repetition of the prayer by Stephen.

Since there is very little ground indeed for Stephen's plea of ignorance on the part of his executioners, it must be that Luke is showing that, after the model of his master, the Christian under persecution or in suffering for Christ's sake must forgive those who inflict the suffering.

The scene of the good thief shows how Jesus, amid the frightful agonies of the cross, still does not lose his tenderness and open-hearted welcome. All the good thief has to do is to recognize his own sinfulness and to acknowledge Jesus as the Christ. It is of course in the former that the difficulty lies, and it is only too attractive to divert even one's own attention (let alone that of others) from oneself by attracting it to the failings of others; then one has company, and at the same time avoids admitting the sin one knows so well.

**21**

## 'KING OF THE JEWS'

*Isaiah 62:1-3, 6-10*

For Zion's sake I will not keep silent,
   and for Jerusalem's sake I will not rest,
until her vindication goes forth as brightness,
   and her salvation as a burning torch.
The nations shall see your vindication,
   and all the kings your glory;
and you shall be called by a new name
   which the mouth of the Lord will give.
You shall be a crown of beauty in the land of the Lord,
   and a royal diadem in the hand of your God.
Upon your walls, O Jerusalem,
   I have set watchmen;
all the day and all the night
   they shall never be silent.
You who put the Lord in remembrance,
   take no rest,
and give him no rest
   until he establishes Jerusalem
   and makes it a praise in the earth.
The Lord has sworn by his right hand
   and by his mighty arm:
"I will not again give your grain
   to be food for your enemies,
and foreigners shall not drink your wine

for which you have laboured;
but those who garner it shall eat it
    and praise the Lord,
and those who gather it shall drink it
    in the courts of my sanctuary."
Go through, go through the gates,
    prepare the way for the people;
build up, build up the highway,
    clear it of stones,
    lift up an ensign over the peoples.


*John 19:19-22*

Pilate wrote a title and put it on the cross; it read,
"Jesus of Nazareth, the King of the Jews." Many of the
Jews read this title, for the place where Jesus was
crucified was near the city; and it was written in Hebrew,
in Latin, and in Greek. The chief priests of the Jews
then said to Pilate, "Do not write, 'The King of the
Jews,' but, 'This man said, I am the King of the Jews.' "
Pilate answered, "What I have written I have written."


## Reflection

Jesus had said that when he was lifted up he would draw
all men to himself, and now he is truly a sign to all
men. It was the custom to fix a placard carrying the
title of the offence on the executed criminal's cross, as a
warning to others. As the execution took place beside
the main road leading out of the city to the west there
would be a considerable number of passers-by; according
to the synoptic gospels they mock Jesus on the cross,
but in John they merely read the title of Christ's
triumph; for this is his moment of victory when he is
finally proclaimed as king. What Pilate's motives were

we can only speculate — did he want to spite the Jews who had so manipulated him, or was this his own tribute to the man whose personality had so impressed him? — but the title, written in all the languages of the known world, can be read as a declaration of Christ's kingship to all nations. This, then, is the fulfilment of the prophecies of Isaiah proclaiming that salvation for all nations will come from Jerusalem and that they will stream to Jerusalem to seek it.

The movement of the passion corresponds to Isaiah's prophecy of the suffering Servant of the Lord, who was to be humiliated and persecuted and by means of this to achieve vindication for himself and salvation for others. Here one sees most vividly juxtaposed both sides of this coin: while the other evangelists describe the mockery and contempt poured on Jesus on the cross, the jibes at his claim to be Messiah and Saviour, 'if he is the son of God, let him save himself', John already sees him enthroned in the majesty which his crucifixion will gain for him. For John the crowds are silent and awestruck. Even on the human level it is by suffering and humiliation borne with patience that a man may reach, and be seen to reach, his full human stature and dignity — 'made perfect by suffering', as the letter to the Hebrews has it — and in Christ's case this is translated onto a higher plane by his perfect, divine obedience to the will of the Father.

**22**

## THE GARMENTS

*Psalm 22:16-21*

Yea, dogs are round about me;
    a company of evildoers encircle me;
    they have pierced my hands and feet —
I can count all my bones —
    they stare and gloat over me;
they divide my garments among them,
    and for my raiment they cast lots.
But thou, O Lord, be not far off!
    O thou my help, hasten to my aid!
Deliver my soul from the sword,
    my life from the power of the dog!
Save me from the mouth of the lion,
    my afflicted soul from the horns of the wild oxen!

*John 19:23-24*

When the soldiers had crucified Jesus they took his garments and made four parts, one for each soldier; also his tunic. But the tunic was without seam, woven from top to bottom; so they said to one another, "Let us not tear it, but cast lots for it to see whose it shall be." This was to fulfil the scripture,

    "They parted my garments among them,

and for my clothing they cast lots."
So the soldiers did this.

## Reflection

The soldiers in charge of an execution normally received
the clothes of the victim and his other personal posses-
sions as part of their recognized 'rake-off'. The
evangelists see in this distribution another fulfilment of
the long psalm to which so many details of the passion-
narrative correspond. By his concentration on the seamless tunic, John alludes to Christ's priestly role; for the
high priest too had a seamless garment. The awaited
messiah was to be not only king but also priest, and John
shows Jesus at the climax of his work in both these roles.
As the Christian apologists of the first generation were
to see, the levitical priesthood of Aaron had been found
to be barren, and Jesus founds this new perfect priesthood. The temple and cult of Israel, genuine vehicle of
worship though it had been for so long, was now super-
seded by the temple of Christ's body, just as the victims
of the old sacrificial rites had given place to the new
and perfect victim.

All these themes, temple, victim, priest, king, people
of God, are concentrated on one fine point. And yet by
means of the body of Christ this is a fine point which
yet fans out to include a whole multitude. In his role
as victim and priest he offers the whole of his body, that
is the whole Christian people in so far as they are united
to him and prepared to offer themselves with him —
and only so far are we genuinely members of his body.
At the same time we are the royal priesthood, offering
Christ to the Father, freed from the role of helpless
and passive beneficiaries, and given an active function
in union with Christ by means of the priesthood which
he grants us all to share.

The seamless tunic has also since the earliest ages been regarded as the symbol of the oneness of Christianity, the impossibility of its being divided. At all but the deepest level the disunity of Christendom is so obvious as to make this a tragic condemnation. Recently a well-informed non-Christian used the strife aroused by the opposition between the different sects as a dissuader from becoming a Christian. But at the deepest level we cannot but be one, simply by the fact of being followers of Christ; if only we could realize it, and drop our dissensions.

**23**

# MARY

*Lamentations 2:13, 15-18*

What can I say for you, to what compare you,
   O daughter of Jerusalem?
What can I liken to you, that I may comfort you,
   O virgin daughter of Zion?
For vast as the sea is your ruin;
   who can restore you? . . .
All who pass along the way
   clap their hands at you;
they hiss and wag their heads
   at the daughter of Jerusalem;
"Is this the city which was called
   the perfection of beauty,
   the joy of all the earth?"
All your enemies
   rail against you;
they hiss, they gnash their teeth,
   they cry: "We have destroyed her!
Ah, this is the day we longed for;
   now we have it; we see it!"
The Lord has done what he purposed,
   has carried out his threat;
as he ordained long ago,
   he has demolished without pity;
he has made the enemy rejoice over you,

and exalted the might of your foes.
Cry aloud to the Lord!
  O daughter of Zion!
Let tears stream down like a torrent
  day and night!
Give yourself no rest,
  your eyes no respite!


*John 19:25-27*

Standing by the cross of Jesus were his mother, and his
mother's sister, Mary the wife of Clopas, and Mary
Magdalene. When Jesus saw his mother, and the disciple
whom he loved standing near, he said to his mother,
"Woman, behold, your son!" Then he said to the disciple, "Behold, your mother!" And from that hour the
disciple took her to his own home.


## Reflection

These two figures are types. Mary is the daughter of
Sion, the mother of the chosen people because she is
mother of Christ whose body is the Church, and also
because she is the first and most perfect of Christians,
the model and the matrix of Christians. The beloved
disciple (he is never named, and this must be deliberate;
he is only presumed to be John) is also in his way the
model of Christians. When he appears he is the model
of love: at the supper he is the disciple whom Jesus
loves, especially close to him by this love; at the empty
tomb he is the first to understand and believe because
he has the understanding born of love. So he stands
simply for the type of the disciple whom Jesus now and
for ever loves, the perfect disciple, model of others. In
this scene, then, the disciple of Jesus down the ages, the

member of the Church, is presented to the mother of the Church and put under her care. It is the basis for those ancient mediaeval statues where Mary is shown protecting the faithful in the shelter of her outstretched mantle.

Here also is the basis for the theology of Mary's part in our redemption. She appears rarely in the gospels: at the beginning of all she gives her consent, a simple country girl in her early teens, welcoming the work of God in a mystified openness to what God will send her. In John she reappears at the first miracle of Jesus at Cana, when he manifests his glory at her instigation, and the disciples first come to believe in him, though his 'hour' has not yet come. And finally now, when his 'hour' is fulfilled she is again at his side, offering herself with him, the mother now not merely of Jesus but of his body, the Church. As such she represents, with the beloved disciple, the union of the whole Church in her Son's offering. By the open-ended, unlimited gift of herself and the disciple to each other she is left standing at the foot of the cross as a symbol and a reality down the ages.

**24**

# THE LAST CRY

*Psalm 22:1-11, 22-31*

My God, my God, why hast thou forsaken me?
    Why art thou so far from helping me,
    from the words of my groaning?
O my God, I cry by day, but thou dost not answer;
    and by night, but find no rest.
Yet thou art holy,
    enthroned on the praises of Israel.
In thee our fathers trusted;
    they trusted, and thou didst deliver them.
To thee they cried, and were saved;
    in thee they trusted, and were not disappointed.
But I am a worm, and no man;
    scorned by men, and despised by the people.
All who seek me mock at me,
    they make mouths at me, they wag their heads;
"He committed his cause to the Lord;
      let him deliver him,
    let him rescue him, for he delights in him!"
Yet thou art he who took me from the womb;
    thou didst keep me safe upon my mother's breasts.
Upon thee was I cast from my birth,
    and since my mother bore me thou hast been my God.
Be not far from me,
    for trouble is near

and there is none to help. . . .
I will tell of thy name to my brethren;
    in the midst of the congregation I will praise thee:
You who fear the Lord, praise him!
    all you sons of Jacob, glorify him,
    and stand in awe of him, all you sons of Israel!
For he has not despised or abhorred
    the affliction of the afflicted;
and he has not hid his face from him,
    but has heard, when he cried to him.
From thee comes my praise in the great congregation;
    my vows I will pay before those who fear him.
The afflicted shall eat and be satisfied;
    those who seek him shall praise the Lord!
    May your hearts live for ever!
All the ends of the earth shall remember
    and turn to the Lord;
and all the families of the nations
    shall worship before him.
For dominion belongs to the Lord,
    and he rules over the nations.
Yea, to him shall all the proud of the earth bow down;
    before him shall bow all who go down to the dust,
    and he who cannot keep himself alive.
Posterity shall serve him;
    men shall tell of the Lord to the coming generation,
and proclaim his deliverance to a people yet unborn,
    that he has wrought it.


*Mark 15:33-37*

When the sixth hour had come, there was darkness over the whole land until the ninth hour. And at the ninth hour Jesus cried with a loud voice, "Eloi, Eloi, lama sabachthani?" which means, "My God, my God, why hast thou forsaken me?" And some of the bystanders hearing it said, "Behold, he is calling Elijah." And one ran and, filling a sponge full of vinegar, put it on a reed and gave it to him to drink, saying, "Wait, let us see whether Elijah will come to take him down." And Jesus uttered a loud cry, and breathed his last.

## Reflection

There are different traditions about Jesus' last cry on the cross; it seems that originally it was simply a great cry (as at the end of Mark's account); but this was later interpreted in different ways. Luke gives a prayer of perfect resignation and acceptance, drawn from the psalms, which had presumably formed the chief part of Jesus' prayer throughout his life. The great cry recorded by Mark and Matthew is more difficult to interpret. At first sight it seems a cry of dereliction, and has been regarded as a sign of the utter darkness which Jesus suffered on the cross, the pain of separation from God, which he underwent on our behalf. But it is in fact the first verse of the psalm to which so many details of the passion correspond; the use of this first verse brings in the psalm as a whole, and the vital truth here is that the psalm ends in triumph: God hears the cry of distress and comforts the sufferer; but perhaps more important, by the suffering undergone glory is brought to God and all peoples are reconciled to him. It is, then, a protestation of faith and hope in the redemptive power of the cross: here, at the moment of his greatest agony, Jesus can still know that his sacrifice will bring glory to God and salvation to the world.

The evangelists are all reticent about the actual process of the crucifixion and death of the Lord. They concentrate rather on the attendant circumstances, and interpret them because they give the profound theological sense of what was happening far more than the recital of the bare facts of crucifixion. These details were, in any case, all too familiar in the Roman world. It was a punishment reserved for slaves, which made even the tough and callous Romans quail. Even the theological accounts of the evangelists, paying the scantest attention to the physical details, still leave the impression of the agonizing torture which wrung the final great cry from Jesus, and the sense of repose and relief when at last death arrives to free him from his struggle.

**25**

# THE SPIRIT

*Ezechiel 37:1-14*

The hand of the Lord was upon me, and he brought me out by the Spirit of the Lord, and set me down in the midst of the valley; it was full of bones. And he led me round among them; and behold, there were very many upon the valley; and lo, they were very dry. And he said to me, "Son of man, can these bones live?" And I answered, "O Lord God, thou knowest." Again he said to me, "Prophesy to these bones, and say to them, O dry bones, hear the word of the Lord. Thus says the Lord God to these bones: behold, I will cause breath to enter you, and you shall live. And I will lay sinews upon you, and will cause flesh to come upon you, and cover you with skin, and put breath in you, and you shall live; and you shall know that I am the Lord."

So I prophesied as I was commanded; and as I prophesied, there was a noise, and behold, a rattling; and the bones came together, bone to its bone. And as I looked, there were sinews on them, and flesh had come upon them, and skin had covered them; but there was no breath in them. Then he said to me, "Prophesy to the breath, prophesy, son of man, and say to the breath, Thus says the Lord God: Come from the four winds, O breath, and breathe upon these slain, that they may live." So I prophesied as he commanded me, and the breath came into them, and they lived, and stood upon their feet, an exceedingly great host.

Then he said to me, "Son of man, these bones are the whole house of Israel. Behold, they say, 'Our bones are dried up, and our hope is lost; we are clean cut off.' Therefore prophesy, and say to them, Thus says the Lord God: Behold, I will open your graves, and raise you from your graves, O my people; and I will bring you home into the land of Israel. And you shall know that I am the Lord, when I open your graves, and raise you from your graves, O my people. And I will put my Spirit within you, and you shall live, and I will place you in your own land; then you shall know that I, the Lord, have spoken, and I have done it, says the Lord."

*John 19:30*

When Jesus had received the vinegar, he said, "It is finished"; and he bowed his head and gave up his spirit.

## Reflection

To describe the death of Jesus John uses one of those fascinating and tantalising expressions which have two senses: 'he breathed his last' or 'he breathed out'. Coupled with the solemn 'it is completed' the phrase is clearly much more than a mere expression of Jesus' death. Breath and spirit are the same word in both Hebrew and Greek, and John means to say that in dying Jesus breathed out on his disciples and the world the promised spirit. This is why the solemn act of his passion, begun with the promises of the Spirit at the last supper, is complete. For Luke the coming of the Spirit occurs at Pentecost, but in John the era of the Church, and so the era of the Spirit has already begun.

When the risen Christ appears on the Sunday evening in the upper room he again breathes on the apostles and gives them power to forgive sins: when he meets them by the lake of Galilee in the early morning he celebrates the Eucharist with them. So the completion of Christ's final act of giving is the giving of the Spirit, because this gift of the Spirit sets the stage for the era of the Church when the Spirit takes the place of Christ's physical presence in the Church. By this he achieves the work which the Father gave him to do. This is the resurrection of the people of Israel at the breath of God of which Ezekiel spoke.

The analogy between spirit and life can be useful also in the Church: when Jesus breathes out his spirit he gives life to the Church. In the primitive Church the manifestation of the Spirit was in extraordinary and unpredictable power and life. Where the Spirit is, there is life, the life-force released by the death of Jesus. This is one of the marks of the Church, remarked by Newman in the power to develop. It is the power to grow and adapt, the power to assimilate or react. In us individuals too the Spirit is a power of life, freshness and vigour; if we are stale and lifeless, it is the Spirit, the power of the risen Christ, that we need.

**26**

## THE FIRST FRUITS

*Isaiah 45:14, 18-19, 22-25*

Thus says the Lord:
"The wealth of Egypt and the merchandise of Ethiopia,
    and the Sabeans, men of stature,
shall come over to you and be yours,
    they shall follow you;
    they shall come over in chains and bow down to you.
They will make supplications to you, saying:
    'God is with you only, and there is no other,
    no god beside him'. . . .
For thus says the Lord,
who created the heavens
    (he is God!),
who formed the earth and made it
    (he established it;
he did not create it a chaos,
    he formed it to be inhabited!):
"I am the Lord, and there is no other.
I did not speak in secret,
    in a land of darkness;
I did not say to the offspring of Jacob,
    'Seek me in chaos.'
I the Lord speak the truth,
    I declare what is right. . . .
"Turn to me and be saved,

all the ends of the earth!
For I am God, and there is no other.
By myself I have sworn,
from my mouth has gone forth in righteousness
a word that shall not return:
'To me every knee shall bow,
every tongue shall swear.'
"Only in the Lord, it shall be said of me,
are righteousness and strength;
to him shall come and be ashamed,
all who were incensed against him.
In the Lord all the offspring of Israel
shall triumph and glory."


*Matthew 27:51-54*

And behold, the curtain of the temple was torn in two, from top to bottom; and the earth shook, and the rocks were split; the tombs also were opened, and many bodies of the saints who had fallen asleep were raised, and coming out of the tombs after his resurrection they went into the holy city and appeared to many. When the centurion and those who were with him, keeping watch over Jesus, saw the earthquake and what took place, they were filled with awe, and said, "Truly this was the Son of God!"


## Reflection

The immediate results of the death of Jesus are symbolic of its effects; here again the evangelists do not pause on the fact of his death, but hasten to interpret it. The rending of the veil of the temple signifies the end of Judaism as the chosen people; after all God's loving care, continually drawing them back to himself, they have finally rejected his Christ. Correspondingly, it is at this moment that the first of the gentiles is converted; the centurion and his company are drawn to acknowledge Jesus as Son of God, and in this they are clearly set over against the Jews who had failed. But between these two Matthew alone relates this scene of the foretaste of the general resurrection. It is perhaps from this that the ancient ikons of Christ drawing the patriarchs from their tombs have their origin; as soon as he descends to the underworld he brings them out by the hand. At all events the evangelist cannot wait till Christ's own resurrection to tell of those who have been waiting for Christ's redeeming death.

This eagerness gives a glimpse of the natural immediacy of the resurrection of Christians after Christ's death. As he has died and risen again there is, so to speak, a sort of in-built impetus in the Christian dead towards the full resurrection. The Hebrew mind, and so the Christian instinct too, cannot envisage a resurrection which is not the resurrection of the body. Life is life in the body as a totality, and the resurrection too must make a total person. The state of the dead before the resurrection must be an unnatural one which could not be the final state. This affirmation of the evangelist, then, with which he concludes his account of Christ's passion and crucifixion by leading on without pause to the resurrection of the dead in Christ, strengthens our hope for the future. The state between death and resurrection is but a moment, a transition, which issues in the grasp of Christ drawing to the fullness of life.